SPACE SUIT

Lots of love, Nora

FIG 2

ROVER

FIG. 3

To all who've paved the way, thank you. And to future generations, dream your own dreams and shoot for the stars. (NP)

For my Starman, Jason. (JF)

First published 2019 by
The O'Brien Press Ltd,
12 Terenure Road East, Rathgar, Dublin 6, D06 HD27, Ireland.
Tel: +353 1 4923333; Fax: +353 1 4922777
E-mail: books@obrien.ie; website: www.obrien.ie.
The O'Brien Press is a member of Publishing Ireland.

ISBN: 978-1-78849-100-6

Text © copyright Norah Patten 2019
Illustrations © copyright Jennifer Farley 2019
Copyright for typesetting, layout, editing, design © The O'Brien Press Ltd.

All rights reserved.

No part of this publication may be reproduced or utilised in any form or by any means, electronic or mechanical, including photocopying, recording or in any information storage and retrieval system, without permission in writing from the publisher.

10 9 8 7 6 5 4 3 2 1
24 23 22 21 20 19

Printed by L&C Printing Group, Poland.
The paper in this book is produced using pulp from managed forests.

SHOOTING for the STARS

By Norah Patten
Illustrations by Jennifer Farley

THE O'BRIEN PRESS
DUBLIN

CONTENTS

About Dr. Norah — 3
Where it all began — 4

The Great Beyond
What is space? — 8
What is an astronaut? — 10
Space programs — 12

Journey to the Stars
Preparing for space — 14
Getting to space — 16
Journey to the ISS — 18

Up, Up and Away
Living in space — 20
Food in space — 22
Fitness in space — 24
What is a spacesuit? — 26
Spacewalks — 28
Experiments in space — 30
Where else do astronauts go? — 32

Closer to Home
Back on earth — 34
Where to next? — 36
The Artistic Astronaut: Nicole Stott — 38
Into the future — 40

Hi, I'm Norah!

I am obsessed with space and exploration and rockets. And I want to go to space! In fact, since I was eleven years old I've wanted to go to space, and I have done everything possible to make that happen.

I grew up in a town called Ballina (that's in County Mayo), the youngest of five children. I have always loved sports; when I was in primary school I trained as a gymnast, and in secondary school I was a swimmer. Now I am training to go to space, and I want to share my journey with you all. I am a citizen scientist-astronaut candidate with Project PoSSUM – I'll explain what that means later, but for now let me tell you a little bit about this book!

Over the years, I have studied a lot, travelled to many different countries, and had lots of interesting conversations with people about space, exploration and how I might someday make my dream a reality. I'll tell you all about how I went from growing up in Mayo to having a space career and training that will allow me to someday – hopefully! – travel into space.

I will share with you what I have learned: how astronauts get to space, what it is like to live, eat and sleep there, and what you need to do to join me up among the stars!

Norah

WHERE IT ALL BEGAN

It all started when I was eleven years of age, in 1995. I had just finished 5th class in Ballina, County Mayo, and I was very excited. Why was I excited? Well, because that summer I was going on an aeroplane for the first time!

My mother's sister and my father's cousins invited us to visit them in Cleveland, Ohio. My first time on an aeroplane AND my first time going to America! When we arrived there, we went to an outdoor swimming pool and lots of big shopping malls ... But I wasn't very interested in shopping or clothes – I was interested in adventure and exploring the outdoors.

One day, my cousin brought us to a place called NASA – it was so amazing! NASA is an organisation that looks after the American space program. They select and train the American astronauts and do lots of research to help us understand as much as possible about space. They also designed and built rockets including the Saturn V, the one that took men to the moon.

I walked around different aircraft and even got to stand beside a spacecraft that had flown in space. That was when I realised I wanted to learn as much as I could about space exploration: How did people travel to

Age 11 at NASA

Age 16

Age 15, with my brother in the rocket garden

Age 17, my space bedroom!

4 SHOOTING FOR THE STARS

space? How did rockets launch off our planet? What happens to your body in space? Could I someday go there?

My dad's cousin Jack also took us to see a movie called *Apollo 13*. It's about a space mission in 1970 that was sending three astronauts to the moon in the Saturn V rocket. There was an explosion on board that damaged the spacecraft, but thankfully the three astronauts made it back home to Earth. After watching this movie, I realised that travelling to space is not easy – and it is dangerous!

Saturn V

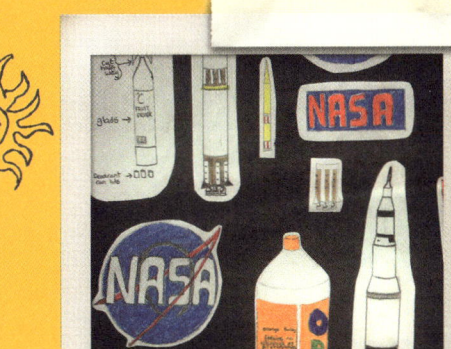
Junior Cert project

I had absolutely no idea how to have a career in space, but I was determined to make it happen. We didn't have the internet at home when I was growing up, so one day I posted a letter to NASA to ask them how I could get a job working for them and what I should study and … THEY REPLIED!

They told me there are many ways to get involved in the space industry, and to start I should consider becoming a pilot or studying engineering, mathematics, science or medicine.

1998: Reply from NASA

WHERE IT ALL BEGAN 5

I saved up my babysitting money to buy my first telescope when I was fourteen. I couldn't see many stars from my house in Ballina, but I could occasionally see some of the moons of Jupiter as tiny specks. I spent a lot of time looking at courses to study in university and decided on aeronautical engineering. I wanted to learn about aircraft and what made them fly – and I noticed that a lot of astronauts had studied this course too.

Ready for takeoff

Ejection seat

PhD Graduation!

After my Leaving Certificate, I was accepted to the University of Limerick (UL), where I studied aeronautical engineering for four years. It was hard work, particularly in first year, but it was worth putting in the long hours.

I continued my studies at UL for another few years, working really hard to get my PhD. But I also knew that it was important to be on the lookout for space-related programs and courses. In 2010, I studied at the International Space University (yes, it is a real thing!), learning all about space and meeting astronauts and space professionals from all over the world. I loved it!

Conference time

Me in my spacesuit

Since then, I've worked at the International Space University as part of the Space Studies Program and travelled to many countries around the world. I worked at the Irish Composites Centre at UL, where I learned more about engineering and led some really cool projects. I even organised the first student experiment from Ireland to go to the International Space Station (ISS). I am now part of a citizen scientist-astronaut program called Project PoSSUM (Polar Suborbital Science in the Upper Mesosphere), doing intensive testing and training and conducting research that will benefit future space missions. I am planning to get to space myself someday, but for now, let me tell you some of the things I have found out so far!

Orion

Me + astronaut Chris Hadfield

Space Wall

WHERE IT ALL BEGAN 7

WHAT IS SPACE?

I used to ask this question a lot when I was growing up. Well, right now we are on a planet called Earth – and Earth is actually in space! Our solar system is made up of our Sun, eight planets including Earth, and other objects that orbit the Sun like rocks, asteroids and comets.

Venus

Earth

Mercury

Mars

There are many ways to study space without sending humans up there. Telescopes are used to look at distant stars and systems, to help us understand how and when they were formed. Probes, rovers and satellites are built here on Earth and launched into space in a rocket, sometimes travelling a long, long way to study the other planets in our solar system.

Saturn

Neptune

Jupiter

Uranus

The first satellite, *Sputnik*, went into space in 1957. It was the size of a beach ball, and it sent a 'beep, beep, beep' radio signal back to Earth for twenty-one days, until the batteries stopped working!

Our Sun is a star, just like the stars we see at night. Stars are bright balls of gas, held together by their own gravity. Our Sun is so huge that more than one million Earths would fit inside it!

WHAT IS AN ASTRONAUT?

An astronaut is a space traveller. Astronauts are very skilled in their fields and have a particular area of expertise to bring to a space mission. They will usually have studied science, technology, engineering, maths, medicine, or they will be a fighter pilot. They rehearse and practise many parts of the mission over and over again on Earth before launching to space so they know what to do once they get there, and also what to do if something goes wrong or if there is an emergency.

I've asked astronauts their advice on what it really takes to succeed, and they told me you need to start preparing as early as possible, in school and also outside school. Astronauts are very good at working in teams and communicating with other people; they are fit and healthy; and often they have hobbies like swimming, running, scuba diving and exploring.

My own journey so far: I studied aeronautical engineering at the University of Limerick and then completed the Space Studies Program at the International Space University. Right now, I am preparing for a commercial spaceflight with Project PoSSUM. We are learning how to take measurements of special clouds (called noctilucent clouds) that are located high up in our atmosphere. We will fly on commercial suborbital spaceflights as scientist-astronauts, hopefully in a few years' time!

SPACE PROGRAMS

Space exploration is often international, meaning different countries work together. Ireland is a member of the European Space Agency (ESA), along with over twenty other countries. Through ESA, companies and organisations work on projects like building rockets, different types of space research, exploring other planets, and studying Earth from space. I have met Irish researchers working at ESA on super-cool space projects – maybe that could be you someday!

Other space agencies include NASA in the United States, JAXA in Japan, CSA in Canada, Roscosmos in Russia, ISRO in India and CNSA in China. European astronauts are selected and trained by ESA, and they launch to the International Space Station (ISS) – along with astronauts from other space agencies – on a Russian-built rocket called the Soyuz. The ISS is a research lab in which astronauts perform experiments in weightless conditions. It is the largest human-made object in space, about the size of a football field, and it took many years to build, with many countries working together to achieve this.

Even though there hasn't yet been an Irish astronaut in space, there have been astronauts with Irish roots. I had the great pleasure of meeting NASA astronaut Eileen Collins in 2006; she is one of my heroes. Eileen was the first woman to pilot and command a space shuttle, and when I spoke with her, she told me her father's family came from County Cork. And although Chris Hadfield is not from Ireland, while his daughter was studying in Trinity College, Dublin, he tweeted the first ever message *as gaeilge* from space! Pretty cool!

PREPARING FOR SPACE

Astronauts spend years training and preparing before they launch into space. They need to be physically fit and healthy for a start.

Next, they train in different locations, like caves and forests, to learn survival skills and how best to work as part of a team. They work with engineers, scientists and other astronauts to complete simulations (pretend space missions) and training exercises. Then, they practise all the different parts of the mission to make sure they are ready once they get to space.

Did you know that astronauts prepare for spacewalks in one of the largest indoor swimming pools in the world? Operated by NASA, it is called the Neutral Buoyancy Laboratory (NBL) and it is in Houston, Texas. Astronauts spend hours underwater in their spacesuits, practising the tasks that need to be done on a spacewalk.

In the NBL, a combination of weights and floatation devices is used to make the astronaut 'hover' under water – neither sinking nor floating upwards – which is similar to the weightless environment in space. The NBL is 62m long, 31m wide and 12m deep, and it contains 23.5 million litres of water – that is really large!

I experienced neutral buoyancy when I did my scuba diving training. Scuba diving is when you have a tank of air on your back to allow you to breathe underwater. Scuba diving is really important for all aspiring astronauts because, if you think about it, it's a really good simulation of being in space.

GETTING TO SPACE

So you might be thinking that someday you would like to take a trip to space. But how will you get there?

Well, astronauts travel to space on a rocket. This is a very powerful machine designed to blast off from a launch pad, reaching great speeds to push away from Earth. Sometimes rockets are stacked, which means they have more than one 'stage'; when the first stage runs out of fuel, the second stage takes over and continues powering the rocket faster and faster until it reaches orbit – a bit like a relay team!

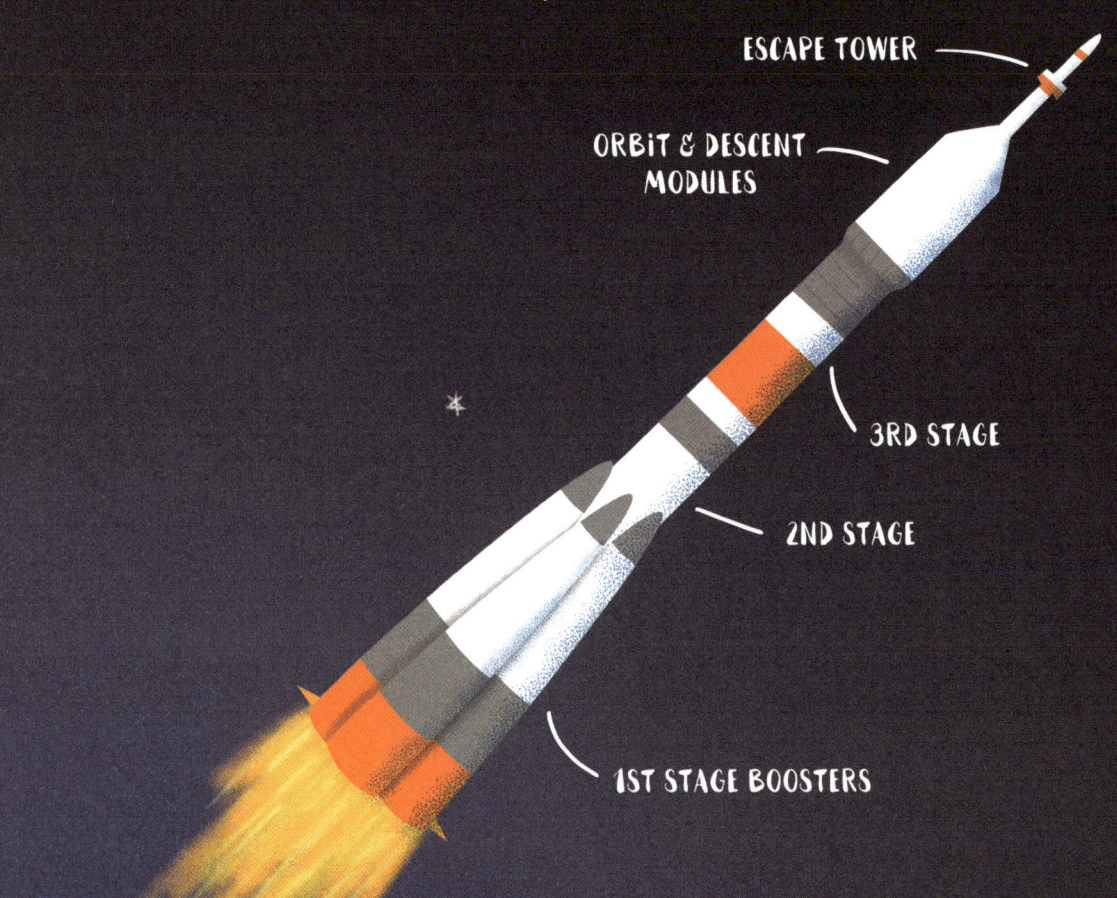

ESCAPE TOWER

ORBIT & DESCENT MODULES

3RD STAGE

2ND STAGE

1ST STAGE BOOSTERS

16 SHOOTING FOR THE STARS

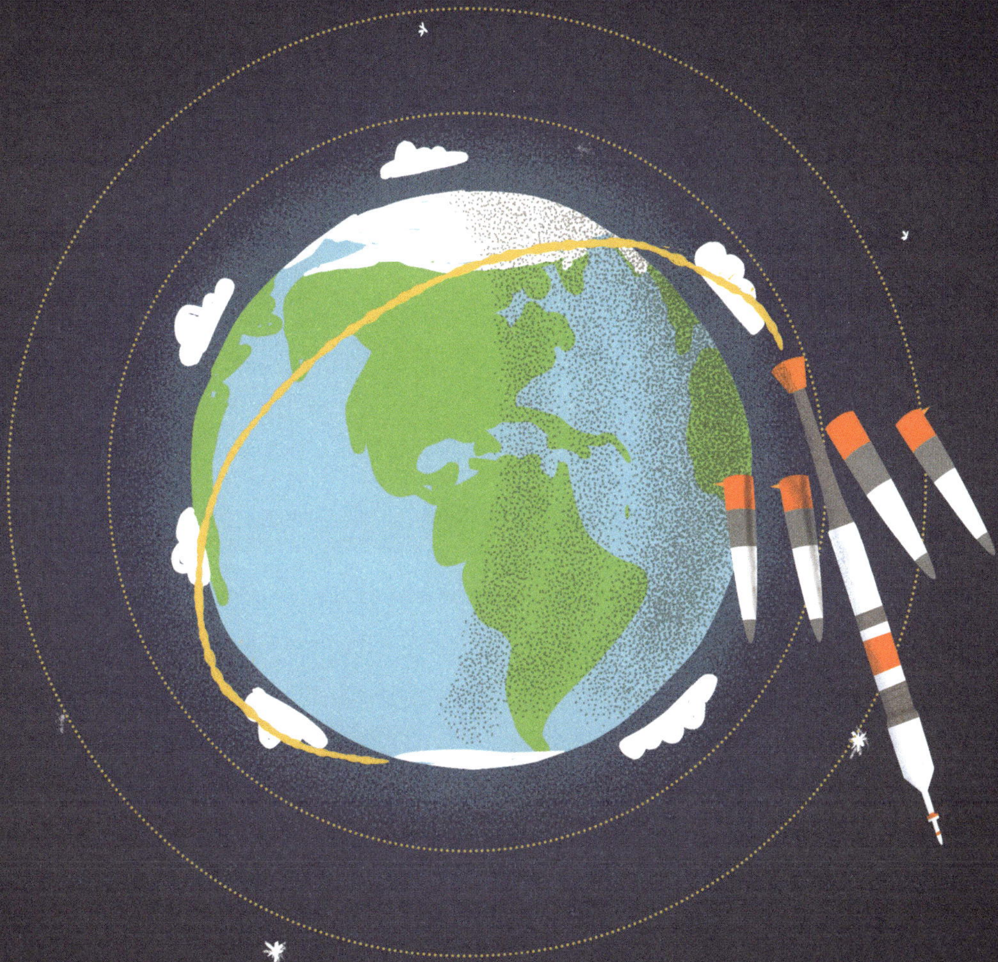

Did you know that space begins 100km above us? That is the distance from my home town, Ballina in County Mayo, to Galway city, which takes around 100 minutes in a car. In a rocket, it takes under three minutes to reach space after lifting off from the launch pad!

JOURNEY TO THE STARS 17

JOURNEY TO THE ISS

Once the rocket blasts off from Earth and reaches orbit, it takes at least another six hours to reach the International Space Station. The rocket has to chase the ISS, reaching the same distance above the Earth and the same speed so that it can dock (attach). Docking is very challenging, and it takes a lot of practice to learn how to do it. Once the rocket docks with the ISS, the astronauts open the hatch and float into their new home, where they will live for the next few months.

Astronauts usually wear a Maximum Absorbency Garment (MAG), which is an adult nappy, under their spacesuit in case they need to go to the toilet on their journey to the ISS. Not very glamorous after all!

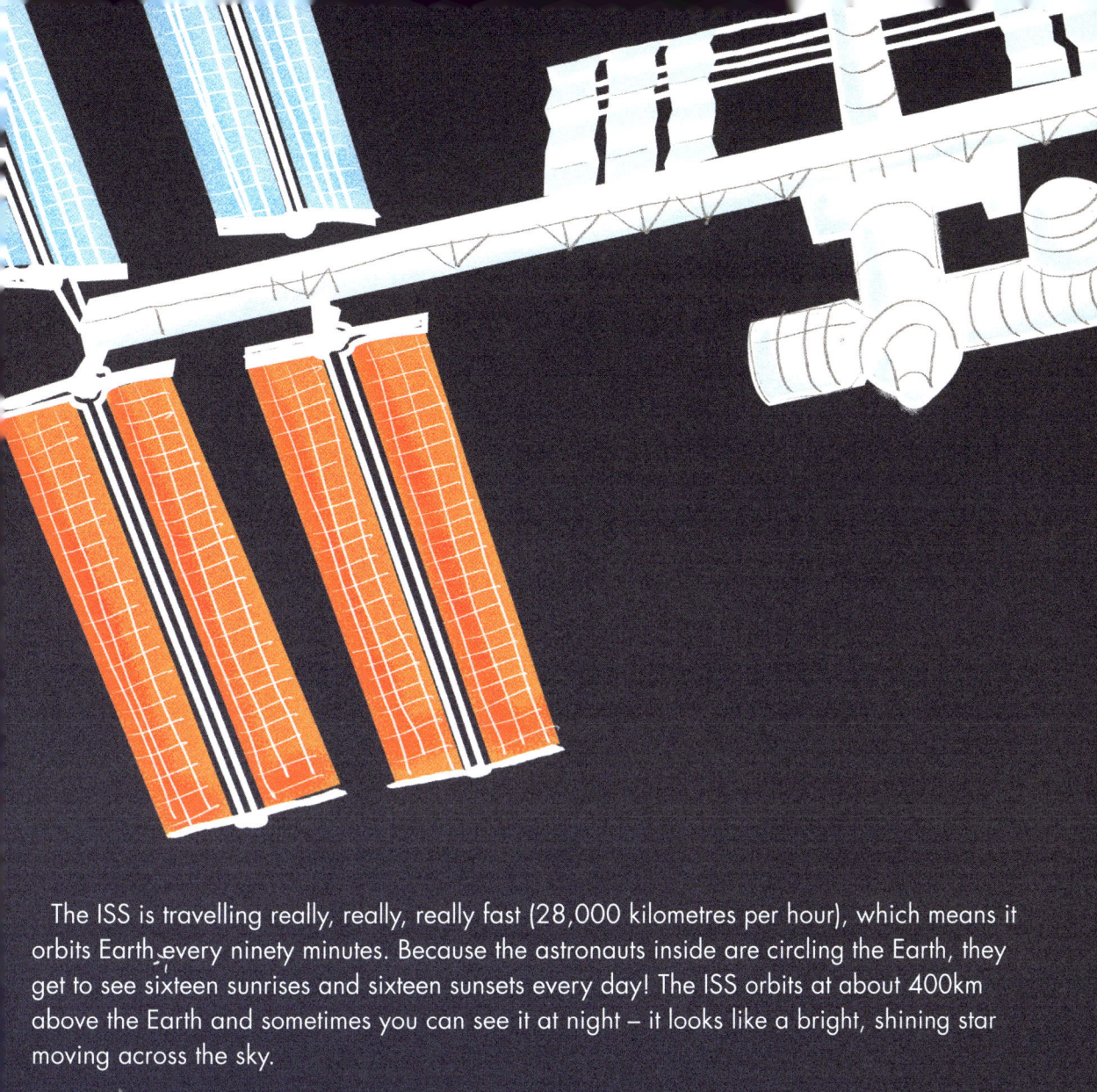

The ISS is travelling really, really, really fast (28,000 kilometres per hour), which means it orbits Earth every ninety minutes. Because the astronauts inside are circling the Earth, they get to see sixteen sunrises and sixteen sunsets every day! The ISS orbits at about 400km above the Earth and sometimes you can see it at night – it looks like a bright, shining star moving across the sky.

LIVING IN SPACE

Astronauts living on the ISS work to an organised and planned schedule. They keep busy doing lots of science experiments, capturing photos of the Earth from space, communicating their experiences and exercising. The temperature on board is kept at around 22°C, so the astronauts often wear shorts, or pants and a t-shirt, while going about their daily duties.

Each astronaut has a tiny bedroom with a sleeping bag attached to the wall. You don't need a pillow in space because everything floats – including your head!

I am often asked how astronauts go to the toilet! Well, for a number one, there is a nozzle on the end of a tube which sucks in the pee for recycling.

For a number two ... it's a little more complicated! There is a seat with a suction pump and a container for the poop. Once finished, the astronaut changes the poop-bag for the next person.

If you could bring three things with you to space, what would they be? I would bring my camera for sure - imagine all those beautiful images of Earth. I would bring a space mission patch designed by Irish students, to represent all the young people in Ireland. Finally, I would take Irish experiments with me so I could do Irish research in space!

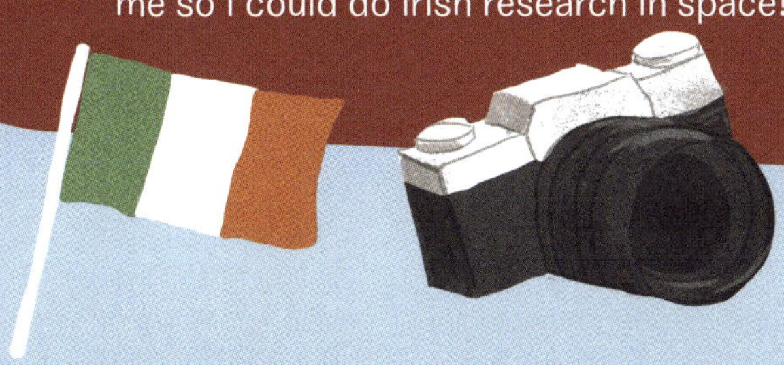

FOOD IN SPACE

I think one of the things I would miss most while living in space is the fresh food we have here on Earth. There are no gardens to grow fruit and vegetables, and no cookers for preparing meals. Instead, food is transported from Earth on a rocket, usually in pouches or cans. This is called a resupply mission, and it also brings clothes, experiments and other equipment. There is enough food stored on the ISS to last a number of months, just in case there are any problems with the resupply missions.

All the food is carefully planned and prepared to make sure astronauts get enough calories and nutrients from each meal. Since everything floats in space, foods like crumbly bread are really bad because the crumbs could float all over the place, even into the computers!

FITNESS IN SPACE

Living in space is not at all like living here on Earth. Instead of walking from one place to another, astronauts simply float. Their muscles have less work to do so they become lazy, and their bones become weaker. This is why it is so important for astronauts to build up their strength by doing lots of exercise before going to space and as part of their daily routines while living up there.

There are three main pieces of exercising equipment on the ISS: a stationary bike with no seat (remember, everything floats in space!); a treadmill for running, with ropes to hold the astronaut down; and weightlifting bars, which are moved around to train different parts of the body.

24 SHOOTING FOR THE STARS

After all that exercise, astronauts need to wash off the sweat. But they can't just shower like we do on Earth because the water would float everywhere and damage the spacecraft! So they use special shampoo on their hair that does not need to be washed out, and on their bodies they use damp cloths and cleaning wipes. Dirty laundry and rubbish from the ISS are placed in a spaceship, which is then destroyed in the Earth's atmosphere.

I keep fit by going to the gym. I enjoy doing different classes like bootcamp and spinning (that's the one on the stationary bike). I try to go three or four times a week, but some weeks I am travelling or doing something else and I might miss a few days – but that's OK!

WHAT IS A SPACESUIT?

There are actually two types of spacesuit. An IVA (intravehicular activity) spacesuit is worn inside the spacecraft during the launch and landing. It gives additional protection to the astronauts if something goes wrong, for example an air leak in the spacecraft. An EVA (extravehicular activity) spacesuit is used outside the spacecraft and is the life-support system for the astronaut during spacewalks. Space is a harsh and dangerous environment: there is no air to breathe, it gets very hot in the sunlight and very cold in the darkness, and the rays from the sun can be harmful because there is no atmosphere like there is here on Earth to protect the astronaut.

As part of Project PoSSUM, I have been testing an IVA spacesuit. When it is 'pressurised', meaning filled with air, it becomes harder to move and work in it. We wear the spacesuit while doing various tasks and then give feedback to the manufacturer on the things that worked well and the things that need to be improved. Our findings will be used to improve the suits for future space missions!

Let's look in more detail at the spacesuit worn for an EVA. It is made up of several parts, including the gloves, helmet, torso (around your chest and stomach) and the lower body. One by one, the parts are clipped together and sealed tight to make sure no air leaks out. There are several different layers of materials in the suit to protect it against impacts – for example being hit by tiny pieces of space debris – and to regulate the temperature, pressure, air and humidity. There is also a communications system in the suit for speaking to the mission controllers throughout the spacewalk.

SPACEWALKS

Just like our homes and cars on Earth, the ISS must be maintained and repaired from time to time. New equipment and experiments need to be installed, and batteries and filters sometimes have to be replaced. To do these jobs outside of the space station, astronauts go on a spacewalk. This is what all those hours of practice in the Neutral Buoyancy Lab were for!

The astronauts change into their protective EVA spacesuits, then they leave the ISS through an airlock. An airlock has two doors: they go through the first door and lock it tight behind them, then they open the second door and float out into space.

The longest spacewalk, by NASA astronauts Jim Voss and Susan Helms, lasted almost nine hours. That would be pretty exhausting, and they wouldn't even get a loo break. We know what that means (the nappy!).

Spacewalkers use special handrails to help them move around from one place to another. They tie themselves to the ISS using tethers, or ropes, to make sure they don't float off into space. Their tool belt is also connected to their spacesuit using a tether. I've been told that spacewalks are very hard work but they are one of the most amazing things to experience. Can you imagine seeing Earth 400km below your feet?

EXPERIMENTS IN SPACE

Did you know that there are many different and exciting experiments happening on the ISS? Research on the human body, plant growth, fire and flames, antibiotics and new medications, materials and how they form, and so much more. Antibiotics and medication work differently in space. Scientists are doing experiments to find out why, so they can make more effective medication for people here on Earth and also for astronauts as we travel farther into space, beyond low earth orbit.

It's fascinating to think how different life is in space because of the lack of gravity. Take fire as an example. When a candle is lighting here on Earth, the hot flame rises from the candle – because hot air likes to rise. But this doesn't happen in space because there is no up or down! Instead, space flames look like circular balls.

In 2014, I organised a competition for secondary school students, asking them to design an experiment to send to the ISS. We received lots of brilliant ideas and entries. We picked one winner, and it became the first student experiment from Ireland ever to be sent to space. And when I get to space, I want to take research being developed in Irish schools and universities.

30 SHOOTING FOR THE STARS

Astronauts use themselves as test subjects, taking blood and muscle samples and monitoring their sleep, eyesight and appetite.

They also grow different plants in space to understand how the roots move into the soil and how they grow without gravity. Astronauts even got to taste the first space-grown lettuce in 2015!

WHERE ELSE DO ASTRONAUTS GO?

When the satellite Sputnik was launched in 1957, there was a race to send humans into space. Yuri Gagarin from Russia became the first human in space in 1961. The American astronauts Neil Armstrong and Buzz Aldrin were the first people to walk on the moon in 1969, after spending three days in their spaceship travelling from Earth.

Humans have not been back to the moon since 1972, but we want to get back there soon! Companies and organisations including NASA are working on rockets that will be able to bring astronauts farther into space, and ESA is also working on a number of projects to understand how we can live and work on the moon.

The Moon: Did you know?

* Gravity on the moon is about one-sixth of what it is on Earth
* It takes about three days to travel to the moon
* The moon does not have any atmosphere
* It takes just over one second for a radio message to get from Earth to the moon (really fast compared to Mars!)

32 SHOOTING FOR THE STARS

Humans have never been to Mars, and right now it is inhabited by rovers sent from Earth to find out what it is like there. Mars is called the Red Planet because it appears reddish-orange due to 'rust' in the Martian rocks and surface. The journey to Mars will take about nine months and once astronauts arrive, there will be a 'communication delay' because it takes about twenty minutes for the signal from Mars to reach Earth – and then another twenty for the reply to reach the astronauts!

These are the people who speak with the astronauts on-board the ISS every day – what a fun job! I learned that there are satellites in space that make this communication possible, kind of like the radio in your car picking up 'radio waves' from different music stations.

CLOSER TO HOME 35

WHERE TO NEXT?

Ever since that trip to NASA when I was eleven, I have been obsessed with space. I've spent a lot of time studying – but hands-on, physical testing and training is just as important. Right now, I am a scientist-astronaut candidate with Project PoSSUM (that's Polar Suborbital Science in the Upper Mesosphere) at the International Institute of Astronautical Sciences. This program is teaching us how to do research and experiments on suborbital spaceflights, which go into space but don't travel around the earth.

So far, through PoSSUM I have done high-g flight training (that is like the force you feel on a roller-coaster when it takes off really fast and you get pushed back in your seat); spacesuit testing and evaluation; hypoxia training (reduced oxygen); spacecraft egress (how to get out of a spacecraft if it makes an emergency landing in water) and research on a microgravity flight (floating weightless, amazing!).

PoSSUM is international and multi-disciplinary, which means participants come from all over the world and from lots of different backgrounds, including medical doctors, engineers (like me!), pilots, scientists and others.

My fellow PoSSUMs and I are hoping to get to space someday soon on a commercial spaceflight. New companies like SpaceX, Blue Origin and Virgin Galactic are developing rockets and launchers that will start taking paying passengers to space in the very near future. And when that time comes, I will be ready!

THE ARTISTIC ASTRONAUT
NICOLE STOTT

I first met NASA astronaut Nicole Stott in the summer of 2012. I loved hearing about her passion for flying, her experiences in space and her plans to use art to inspire others. Here, Nicole tells us a bit about herself and kindly shares some advice!

Tell us about your journey to become an astronaut.
My parents shared what they loved with me: flying and creativity. I studied aeronautical engineering; I also earned my private pilot's license and SCUBA license. I worked for NASA as an engineer on the Space Shuttle and the International Space Station program at the Kennedy Space Center, and as a flight engineer on the Shuttle Training Aircraft at Johnson Space Center.

What is your advice to a young person wanting to become an astronaut?
Always pay attention to the things that excite you and that you're curious about – this will help you find the best path for your studies, your career and your life. It will help you do things that have meaning.

How many times have you flown to space?
Twice. In 2009, I flew to the ISS on the Space Shuttle *Discovery* STS-128 mission, spent over three months there as a member of the Expedition 20 and 21 crews, and returned home on the Space Shuttle *Atlantis* STS-129 mission. In 2011, I returned to the ISS for two weeks on the final flight of the Space Shuttle *Discovery* STS-133.

What is an average day in space like?
Every day is different, a mix of science, maintenance and outreach. Some days I got to fly the robotic arm, and one day I even got to go outside on a spacewalk!

38 SHOOTING FOR THE STARS

What are the best and worst things about living in space?
Worst = not having my family there with me. Best = everything else!

And what did you miss about space once you got home?
Floating, the view out the window, and the work we were doing together up there.

What do you think is the future of space exploration?
It will continue to grow through international cooperation. I see us back on the Moon and establishing a permanent presence there, and also finally continuing on to Mars. Everything we do will ultimately be about improving life here on Earth.

Can you tell us about your space art?
My space art started by actually doing art in space! I painted a watercolour of my favourite picture I had taken from space. Now my art is not only for enjoyment but is also a unique way for me to share my spaceflight experience. I'm combining three of my favourite things, space, art and wellness, and helping kids recognise that they're already in space and on a planet: we are all Earthlings, and we should behave like the crew of spaceship Earth!

Nicole Stott worked for NASA for twenty-seven years and was selected as an astronaut in the year 2000. She retired in 2015 and is now a full-time artist and SciArt education advocate, and founder of the Space for Art Foundation. Find out more at nicolestott.com and spaceforartfoundation.org.

INTO THE FUTURE

Over the years, I have spoken with many astronauts who have been to space and others who have done everything they could possibly do to get there. I've learned many lessons and picked up some valuable information from meeting and working with all these amazing people. Here are some thoughts I would like to share ...

* **The journey has to be as important as the destination.** Getting to space is my ultimate goal in life, but I need to be happy on my journey to get me there! My husband, friends, family, work and hobbies are all really important and need to be looked after.

* **Just because someone tells you something is impossible, that's not a good enough reason not to try.** YOU decide what your big goals and big dreams are, and YOU decide how to try to make them happen.

* **Create your own identity.** If you want to do something different in life, learn from others but don't copy their success. Be yourself.

* **Don't take things for granted because some opportunities may never come by again.** Enjoy the successes and appreciate them for what they are when you have them.

* **Be as kind to yourself as you would be to your best friend.** My sister told me this because sometimes I can be too hard on myself. Give yourself a break! Not everything works out the way you plan it, but that's OK.

As for me, I will continue to pursue my journey to the stars. I will continue to learn and challenge myself and take on new projects. And I will continue to share all of these experiences and adventures with you, hoping that I can inspire you to shoot for the stars too. Because, after all, the sky is not the limit!

Always adventurous, aged 3

Gymnastics!

NASA 2006

Ready for a high-g flight!

Spacesuit testing